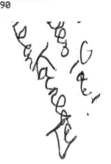

Out of the Darkness into the Light

A Pastor's Miraculous Path to the Pulpit

Leon Kornegay

Copyright © 2019 by Leon Kornegay
All rights reserved.

This book or no parts of this book may be reproduced, transmitted in any form by any means electronic, mechanical, photocopy, recording or otherwise without the written permission from the author.

Unless otherwise noted, scriptures are taken from the King James Version (KJV) public domain

First published in Greensboro, North Carolina

Printed in the United States of America 2019

Cover design: David Terry

ISBN: 978-0-578-46722-1

*"And it came to pass, that, as I made my
journey, and was come nigh
unto Damascus about noon, suddenly
there shone from heaven
a great light round about me...And when
I could not see for the glory
I came unto Damascus...
And one Ananias said unto me...
Brother Saul, receive thy sight...
Arise, and be baptized, and wash away thy sins,
calling on the name of the Lord."*
Acts 22:6, 11a, 13a, 16

Dedication Page

I dedicate this book to my late mother, Anna E. Kornegay, whose love and prayers blessed me throughout my life's journey.

Acknowledgement Page

I would like to thank:

My wife and partner in ministry, Lady Sandra Kornegay, who encouraged me for two years to write this book and then transcribed my thoughts onto paper and helped in innumerable other ways;

Evangelist Beverly D. Allen, who suggested that I consider contacting Jim Murray as my editor;

Elder Jim Murray, his wife, Mae and the Write it Right Editorial Services who labored over the manuscript until its completion.

Foreword

The opportunity to hear life changing testimonies has been vast and varied as an evangelist and a pastor's wife. Such is this testimony of District Elder Leon Kornegay, Pastor of Living Water New Life Ministries. I have come to know both Pastor Leon and Assistant Pastor Sandra Kornegay more intimately over the past 16 years and their openness and transparency to share their journey is a most powerful witness to the saving Grace of Jesus Christ and encouragement to adults and youths who may be experiencing the struggles with an addiction.

Pastor Kornegay preaches the Gospel of Jesus Christ while sharing his story around the country, as well as on local levels, and is one of the boldest and most unashamed witnesses for JESUS CHRIST and His Saving Grace. He will witness and pray in the grocery store, on sidewalks, or wherever an opportunity presents itself. It is a story long overdue. I am so happy that Lady Kornegay has consistently encouraged her husband to put this phenomenal victorious transformation in print for the world and the body of Christ to share as a tool to uplift others who have no hope.

Anyone who meets Pastor Kornegay would never presuppose or detect his former life experiences, because when he was delivered there were no "visual" scars or wounds left that **scream:** I was once struggling with an addiction! This story is nothing short of miraculous. It is also a testimony that the sovereign Lord has a plan for your life (Jeremiah 29:11) and after the cleanup; there is a buildup of relationships that catapult you to where the Lord wants to use you for His Glory.

Proverbs 12:4 states, *"A virtuous woman is the crown of her husband."* Lady Kornegay is without a doubt the "crown Jewel" God gave to him, designed and groomed to be the patient, kind, and prayerfully committed wife he needed that would allow God to direct their course. The dynamic team that they are is immediately recognized after spending a little time in fellowship with them and their faithfulness of service to the call.

This is a story that has been validated over time. The strength of their witness has been tested in the face of adversity and the walk has been more than talk. I am so honored to be able to say they are the real deal and continue to be passionate about their faith in Christ and their call.

We will all be blessed to know their story and know that Jesus Christ the same yesterday, today, and forever is still able to do exceedingly, abundantly above all that we could ask or think.

Evangelist Beverly D. Allen (Author of *"Covenant Dating: The Biblical Path to Marriage," "Good Women in Bad Situations"* and *"No Man's Concubine: Tell the Concubine She was Meant to Be a Queen."*)

Introduction

When I met Leon, he had just given his life to the Lord. And I wasn't aware of his past life. He heard me giving my telephone number to a friend and he wrote it down. Then, he started calling me all the time -- even though I asked him not to. Finally, upon my grandmother's request, I decided to talk to him on the phone.

A few of my church friends encouraged me to go out with him. We went to dinner and I asked my friends to get to the restaurant before me and act like they didn't know we were coming there. Our first date was on March 18, 1980. That was when he told me that I was going to be his wife. I thought he was crazy for even thinking such a thing.

I went to a youth service and Leon was asked to give his testimony. I was happy for his life change. However, I felt that we should have had that conversation first before hearing it in church. As time went on, we continued to date and then on December 18, 1980, he asked me to marry him. I said yes with the intention of a long engagement. My Pastor told us that it wasn't good for saints to have long engagements. In January, 1981, we decided to get married on July 18th. On our honeymoon, I asked Leon if he realized that all three of our dates were on the 18th of the month.

Immediately, Leon began to tell me that although Christ changed his life, he still would follow Muslim eating habits. I told him that I would respect his way of eating but he also had to respect the way I wanted to eat. While dating, I never ordered pork or red meat. I was a person that loved to eat beef, pork, and fish. Leon wanted chicken seven days a week! Eventually, that became a problem, so we met halfway on both sides. I ate more chicken and he started eating beef in moderation.

I had a son from a previous marriage and I was very overly protective of him. I was 18-years-old and had gotten married to a person who had not matured as a man because he was only nineteen. The marriage ended after a year and five months and my son's father wasn't active in his life. When I married Leon, at 27-years-old, I let him know that my son was hurt once by not having a man in his life and I hope that he would fill that void.

Leon didn't really know much about fatherhood because he didn't have a father in his life. One thing my son and Leon had in common was, Leon had his grandfather and my son had his great grandfather. To top things off, I grew up without a father in the home or a male figure. It was just my Mom and her three daughters.

The first two years of our marriage were rough. The first year we were trying to blend our ways together. I grew up all my life in an apostolic church with very strong holiness standards. I didn't go to parties, never smoked cigarettes or drank alcohol. My husband thought because I didn't know anything about the streets, I was naive to worldly things. I used to ask questions about his past and he would say, "Sandra, you wouldn't understand."

In the first three months of our marriage, Leon told me that the Lord called him to the Ministry to preach the Gospel. I was so upset; I would cry myself to sleep. I always said that I didn't want to marry a preacher. Leon began to get so many engagements further and further away from home. After three months of marriage, I also became pregnant with our youngest son.

I was bitter because Leon was working all week and preaching all weekend. And if he wasn't preaching, he was invited to give his testimony. Because I was expecting a child, I was very sensitive and felt very alone. My husband was so full of zeal and just wanted to give to the Lord more than what he gave to the devil. That left me trying to figure out why he got married.

He began to give his testimony so much and I was learning something new every time. Also, I started hearing so many things on television about AIDS and I began to wonder if Leon was infected before he got saved and didn't know it. I didn't know that he had already been tested before he married me.

One day, when I was at my doctor's office for routine blood work, I asked my doctor if they checked for AIDS. He said no. He asked me why I asked that question and I told him because of my husband's past drug addiction. He gave me the papers to sign to consent for the test.

He informed me that the test was negative and then I informed my husband that I had it done. That's when he told me that he had been tested and his was negative also. I was relieved, but upset that I didn't know so much about his drug addict life style. I was learning about different things every time I witnessed his testimony.

After about 20 years of marriage, I asked him is there anything else I needed to know about him. One of his friends that he led to Christ would tell me some of the crazy things they did when they were out there on drugs. I would shake my head in disbelief: that was another story that I had never heard.

I must say after three years of our marriage, each year got better and better. The only complaint I had that I didn't understand was why he wanted to be in church seven days a week. I wanted to spend more time with him. I guess it's because that's what I did as a child and teenager seven days a week. It wasn't what I wanted to do. Yet, I still felt that I loved the Lord just as much as he did. Now, the more he ministers to me and the congregation at the church, I realized that he is just living the life he loves.

For me, living with a former Muslim was more difficult than living with a former drug addict. My husband had to learn that a woman should also have a voice in the home, too. I praise God that I was always an independent strong individual when it came to my beliefs. When I was a little girl, my former pastor always said that if you know the truth, stand on it and don't let anyone change you.

When Leon would say some things he learned in Islam, I would say, "Well that won't work in this house." He would always double check what I would say with his

Pastor. Then, he would come back and say I was right and remind me that he is still learning this Christian walk.

To God be the Glory! It's been almost 38 years and I am so glad that I married him. Many of my church friends told me not to marry him because of his past. Those individuals who told me not to marry Leon are divorced today. Before I married him, I told the Lord if I ever married again; please let him love you so much that it would be easy for him to love a wife.

Lady Sandra Kornegay

Table of Contents

Chapter 1 The Monkey on my Back Grew to be a Gorilla........1

Chapter 2 Sold Out to Allah..13

Chapter 3 College Couldn't Save Me.......................................17

Chapter 4 A New Year's Eve Gift from God..........................21

Chapter 5 Saying "So Long" to Allah....................................25

Chapter 6 The First Time I Gave My Testimony....................29

Chapter 7 Mama, Can I Preach to You?.................................33

Chapter 8 Face to Face With My Father.................................37

Chapter 9 I've Preached and Testified on Good Ground......41

Chapter 10 I'm Doing What I Love!.......................................45

Chapter 11 A Man after God's Own Heart............................49

Chapter 12 It's All About Souls..55

Chapter 13 Raising Children in the Opioid Era......................57

Addendum..61

Chapter 1

The Monkey on my Back Grew to be a Gorilla

I would just like to say, at the time of this writing, I am 66 years old. I make this statement because of my drug addiction, I was told that I would not live past my 27th birthday.

I grew up in an inner city neighborhood on Peshine Avenue in Newark, NJ. It was a nice neighborhood when we first moved in. The majority of the population was black families trying to survive. Most of the families were on welfare assistance and lived in one parent homes; mothers taking care of their children. Everyone looked out for each other and our parents looked out for all the kids. My grandfather was such a financial help to our family, assisting with the bills for the house.

Twelve family members lived in our three bedroom apartment. That was home for my mother, Anna Kornegay and me, my four siblings, an uncle and aunt, cousins and in-laws. It was not easy when we ate, slept and took a bath. You had to wait your turn.

As kids, we used fruit baskets to play basketball by putting the baskets up on a tree. We played stick ball in the streets. We had to stop when cars came through. There would always be fights one day and, we all would be best friends again the next day. Almost every family had a dog and we would watch dog fights all the time.

You would always see the "Number Man," especially at our house. There was one black store in the neighborhood and you played the numbers there. (I don't ever recall hearing that anyone hit the right number).

I attended Charlton Street and Bergen Street Elementary Schools, then Clinton Place Junior High School. There was really nothing wrong at home but that didn't stop me from heading down a wrong path. My behavior went from bad to worse. And it would not end during my time in school.

There weren't many drug addicts back then, but there were so many alcoholics. The stores in the neighborhood were owned by white people. I joined a "gang" called Aztecs that did good things in the neighborhood. The brothers in that group got together and we looked out for each other. Still, we weren't perfect and would go into stores and steal. That was a condition for becoming a member of that gang.

I used to play stickball and basketball with some guys who I saw walking around with white handkerchiefs and brown small paper bags covering their noses. I didn't really know what they were doing at the time. They told me that was a way to get high. They explained that they poured lighter fluid into handkerchiefs and sniffed it to get high. They would also pour airplane glue into a brown paper bag to sniff that to get high. I became curious enough to want to try it. My drug use started at the age of 13. By the time I was 15, I was introduced to pills called seconal, tuminial, black beauties and Quaaludes to get high.

Over time, I was impressionable and wanted to hang out with the older guys who thought they were tough. I was attracted to them. They had the girls. I wanted to be cool like them and I enjoyed that feeling. I also enjoyed going to house parties high. That was what everybody was doing, especially the people I was hanging out with. If you weren't getting high back then, you weren't cool.

My junior year of high school, I was introduced to Heroin and started out sniffing the drug. That was when I left pills alone. I can remember the first time I shot heroin. I vomited so much but I couldn't wait until the next day to shoot some more. I really started using those drugs when I was 17 and battled this problem for 10 years. I felt like the "monkey on my back grew to be a gorilla."

After about six months, I wasn't feeling the high from heroin like I was in the beginning. I was getting sick, vomiting, sweating and I had diarrhea. Some of my "friends" who were already main lining (shooting in their veins), told me that my high would be so much better. That is the trap that drug use sets: you are always looking for a greater high.

In high school at the age 16, I started taken cebas, codeine and drinking cough syrup that was called zilla on the street. I continued going to school and was elected to vice president of the student body. Following in the path of my older brother, I even made the basketball team in junior and senior high. In my junior year, the team won the city, county and state basketball championships. As part of a team, I was a winner but in my personal life, I was still unable to escape destructive behavior. Some members of the team would even sniff drugs in the locker room before our games.

At first, I was skin popping, because I was afraid to shoot in my veins. But skin popping didn't make me feel the way I wanted to feel. Then, I began main lining to get a better high, because that was the high I was looking for. I was told I would enjoy the high much better if I mixed heroin with cocaine. When you mixed heroin and cocaine together, it was called a speed ball. If you took just heroin and you were too low, then you would shoot cocaine to bring you up. If you took the cocaine and you were too high, then you would shoot heroin to bring you down.

That was the story of the addict: you were always trying -- but failing – to experience what you felt on that first high. You go from feeling super to being miserable (sick) a lot of the other times. (The National Institute on Drug Abuse defines addiction as a disease. I guess that's why addicts like me said they were "sick" when going through withdrawals). I can now imagine how I turned into a nasty person who no one wanted to be around during those times.

My addiction was so bad that I had tracks up and down my arms. I had to wear long sleeve shirts even in the summer to cover my arms. It was so bad that my veins had somewhat collapsed and I had difficulty finding a good vein to shoot the drugs into my arms.

Let me tell you: drugs are nothing to play with. I've had guns pointed in my face more than once. Sometimes I robbed people and sometimes I got robbed. I was broke, my car was repossessed and I needed a way to support my addiction. I started selling cocaine to make money, however I didn't make a profit because I was using the drugs myself.

One day, I went to a very bad neighborhood. I took a friend with me to make this deal. I thought this person was my friend so I left him in the car with the cocaine and I only took the drugs with me that I wanted to sell.

When I came back downstairs, my car and friend were gone. When I returned home, the guy I was working for called me and asked how I was doing with my cocaine sales. I told him what happened. He came and picked me up and took me to my friend's house. The guy I was dealing for pulled out a Magnum 357 and put it to my friend's head. My friend said I was lying and that the both of us shot up all the cocaine. The dealer took that same gun from my friend's head and pointed it at mine. He told me if I didn't have his money by a certain date, he was going to hurt me bad.

But drugs were "a big cash only business" and it took over the lives of many in the community. The dealers on the streets of Harlem would not sell any cocaine or other drugs if you were even one dollar short. I mention this because I had messed up with the guy I was selling for, so at this point it was difficult for me to buy drugs with no money.

When I was having withdrawals, I would get up at 5 am in the morning, hoping the drug dealers would be out on the streets. It was an ugly game because drug dealers would talk to you any old way and treat you like dirt. To them, you were nothing but a drug addict – a junkie.

Speaking of my behavior, I started stealing from my loved ones, family members who cared about me. Once, I robbed my brother-in- law to get drugs. However, I didn't know that he knew that I had robbed him. I was on my way to his house the next day. My sister saw me coming and yelled, "Run! Run! He's going to shoot you because he said you robbed him!"

I would like to explain what a shooting gallery is like. It is a room with armed guards at the door. A person would pay $2 to get in and rent space. Sometimes there would be 50 plus people in the room, both male and female. There would be a bowl or a large can on the table with a bunch of needles in it. Everybody would use the same needles over and over. Sometimes they would clean them, using water and other times they would use alcohol. It was a very crazy situation but it became normal to me.

At any time, a stickup man could walk in to rob the place for money and drugs. By the grace of God, that never happened while I was there. There were days when I was sick and didn't have money to buy drugs. I would find a top or spoon that I once used to cook the heroin and I would scrape the cooker to relieve my sickness.

My addiction took over my life and caused me to sleep around and engage in unsafe sex with many women. Back then, I didn't understand the dangers of that kind of reckless behavior but I never contracted any STD, virus or AIDS due to my behavior. To God be the Glory!

Other times when I was sick and didn't have money to buy drugs; I would go to a park in downtown Newark. People on methadone would hang out in this park.

(Methadone is a synthetic opioid prescribed for moderate to severe pain and is commonly used to treat addictions, especially addiction to heroin. It is used to stabilize patients and minimize withdrawal symptoms in the case of an addiction. It has a legitimate legal use but also a high likelihood of its users developing a dependence).

In the park, drug users had a technique called spit back. Addicts from the methadone clinic would drink the methadone and hold it in their mouth. Then, they would spit it back in the bottle and sell it to the drug addicts on the street that were sick. I found myself that desperate because I was so sick and didn't have money for drugs. I did what I had to do.

I can remember getting arrested a number of times. One occasion in particular stands out. It was 1970 and I was 17-years-old. While working in Bamberger's, a Newark department store, I was arrested for shoplifting. I was handcuffed and chained together with 30 other prisoners and put in a bullpen. Everyone who went before the judge that morning was given jail time. I was the last one to go before the judge and I was scared. I had watched as everyone before me was being sent to Jamesburg, a very bad facility back then. I was worried when I finally stood before the judge but he only gave me one-year probation. I didn't know it then, but I know it now: that had to be the Lord.

My car had been repossessed and I had lost my job at General Motors. I got fired because of my drug addiction. I was calling in sick on a regular basis. Someone in Human Resources told me that I was uncivilized and would never work for GM again. While working there as an inspector, I was making $600 a week.

These were the results of my drug habit. I would borrow from loan sharks on the job every day. Then on payday, I had to give them the majority of my paycheck. Whatever I had left, I used to get high. Believe it or not, for much of those first years, I was enjoying getting high tremendously. The pain of withdrawals was part of the cost to pay for the pleasure. It wasn't until the last year that I started having regrets about my addiction.

In 1971, President Nixon declared a "war on drugs." I was a casualty in that war. Despite the resources of federal, state and local enforcement task forces and the highly publicized arrests of black drug kingpins, the flow of drugs increased and lives were being lost on the streets.

I remember a time when I had shot drugs from 7 am to 7 pm. I tried to jump out of a two story window. My friend reached out and pulled me back in. That was just one way drug addiction could literally destroy your life.

Harlem, one of the biggest sites of drug activity in the country, is conveniently just five miles across the Hudson River from Newark. While so-called drug lords like Frank Lucas and Nicky Barnes operated with seeming impunity, they kept up with the cravings of users like me.

Whenever I went over to Harlem, there was an operator who was called the hit man. We had to find him and pay him to hit us (shoot the drugs in our veins). He was the man who could find a vein even if you couldn't.

One time, I was in Harlem in a drug shooting gallery with my friends. An elderly man in his sixties came in and started shooting dope and cocaine. He seemed like he was enjoying his high so much, I told my friends, I can't wait to get that age and be able to shoot dope and cocaine and feel just like that. I was just that hooked and wrapped up in my addiction. I was so addicted that if I heard someone had overdosed, I would start looking for that drug that killed him!

Another time, I ran into a friend who lived in Harlem and was addicted to drugs. He was sick and was having withdrawals and I was sick with withdrawals also. I had just bought a quarter of heroin and he asked me for some, but being sick also, so I told him no. Then, he pulled out a pistol and put it up to my head. His hand was shaking. I gave him what he wanted. I was thankful that he didn't take my life.

During the years I struggled with drugs, addicts were overdosing all around the city (and the country). If it wasn't for the grace of God, I wouldn't be alive to tell my story.

Chapter 2

Sold Out to Allah

*"Thus saith the Lord the King of Israel, and his redeemer the Lord of hosts; I am the first, and I am the last; **and besides me there is no God.**"* Isaiah 44:6 *(emphasis added)*

My cousin, who was in the Nation of Islam (NOI), saw my condition with drug abuse and took me to the Mosque. He told me that there was no other god than Allah and that Allah would change my life. They would teach that Jesus was nothing more than a good man or a prophet.

I was in the Nation of Islam from 1969 to 1979. I received my X, which was Leon 11X. Their teaching especially targeted black men. It was a message that attracted thousands in the inner cities and in prisons. They called the white man the devil, promoted financial independence through home and business ownership to their followers.

One of our primary responsibilities was to provide security whenever we came together at the mosques. Meetings were open to anyone. We might be up on the roof or sitting in cars. However, in my 10 years being a member of the Nation of Islam, I never stopped getting high, shooting heroin and cocaine.

When we were out in public, we wore suits and bowties and could be readily identified. I was down to one suit. It was green velour and it was my favorite. (When I got saved, I dressed in that same suit every Sunday. What I wore on the outside did not reflect the change in my life on the inside).

One day, I was walking the streets selling my *Muhammed Speaks* newspaper. The paper sold for $1.00 but a donation was also accepted. I wasn't having a good day. On a typical day, I would only sell 20 of the 100 papers I had. I was harassed by the police who would tell me to move along or get off of the corner where I was. Most of those officers were white and some were openly hostile.

(In fact, Newark exploded in riots on July 12, 1967 when a rumor spread that white Newark police officers had beaten a black taxi driver for no cause and the city was seized in five days of violent unrest). I remember bullet holes from that conflict in our front porch.

I came home one day and my mother and some family members were looking at their church on television. I started yelling: "Turn that mess off!" Then I said, "Don't you know what the cross means? It means that the white man is double crossing the black man!"

My mind went back to one of my many scrapes with death when I was in the Nation of Islam. When I got home, I began to pray to Allah. I said, "Allah, if you bring me out this time, I'll never do that again."

But because the addiction was so insane, the next morning I got up and started shooting more drugs. There was no power in the name of Allah, but when I called on the name of Jesus, I never desired to use drugs again. I was delivered and set free immediately.

When I give my testimony about Islam, I receive questions from men who may have been searching for the truth after following Islam at some point in their life. Since I was the person who decided to make Jesus my choice, they wanted to know what made me come to the conclusion that I would serve the Lord.

I would tell them all: whether it was a former Muslim or someone struggling with drugs, I couldn't stop doing drugs and acting like the devil until I accepted **Jesus.**

Chapter 3
College Couldn't Save Me

In 1970, I graduated from high school as an average student. Away from the school, I had been locked up for shoplifting. I had a lawyer who told me, "You need to go to college." I was accepted at Claflin University, one of two HBCU's (Historically Black Colleges and Universities) in Orangeburg, South Carolina. The other was South Carolina State University. I was over 700 miles from home in the South on a college campus with hundreds of mostly African American students. It was a totally different environment.

Claflin was affiliated with the United Methodist Church like other HBCU's which had been started by black churches. The influence of Christian culture was there. Claflin had other students who had come from inner city neighborhoods like mine. Some of them had the same habits that I had. And I was drawn to them. I was not their ideal student. I was convinced that there was one professor who didn't care for inner city students from up north. It didn't help that I still could not overcome my drug habit.

I even tried out for basketball and played on the team for a while. But I didn't last a full year. I grew homesick and came back home defeated, bringing my habit back with me.

Back in New Jersey, I enrolled in Monmouth College (now Monmouth University). My older brother, Ron was an All American basketball player in college and was Monmouth's all-time scoring leader. While he was there, the team reached the NAIA national tournament three times. After graduation, he remained close to the program and would later become the school's head basketball coach and then Assistant Athletic Director.

I believe I was accepted there in part because of my brother. I was at Monmouth on and off for three years. I ended up being arrested on campus for giving drugs to a minor, an underage 16-year-old white girl. I was kicked out during the same time my brother was assistant basketball coach. Needless to say, he was not happy.

I remember one day in my college dorm room, I had gone to my mail box. There was a check for me for $2,400 to pay for my room. The check was made out in my name, so I called one of my friends to pick me up and we went to the bank to cash the check. We went straight to Harlem to buy drugs. Within two days, we had spent all of the $2,400 shooting heroin and cocaine.

Chapter 4

A New Year's Eve Gift from God

"...repent, and be baptized every one of you in the name of Jesus Christ for the remission of sins and you shall receive the gift of the Holy Ghost." Acts 2:38

In 1979, something wonderful happened to me. I was sitting home with no job, no money, my car had been repossessed and I was sick with withdrawals. A young lady named Rosalyn Parchment came to my house to see my aunt Aleyce, who was a seamstress. While she was waiting for my aunt, she started talking to me about Jesus. She didn't know my condition or my situation. She just began to witness about Jesus and invited me to her church. At first, I did not believe her because I was told the same thing about Allah, that he could deliver me and make me free. And that did not happen.

I finally visited her church on New Year's Eve, 1979. It was the first time being inside of a church in many years.

The late Bishop William Abney was preaching a message on how the Lord Jesus Christ can change your life, deliver and set you free. He said, "No matter what you've done, Jesus loves you."

While sitting in church that night, I was sick and having withdrawals because I hadn't used drugs all day. My nose was dripping, my mind was slipping, I had the shakes and body aches. I was miserable. I realized that I was in bondage and headed toward an early death. It seemed like he was preaching directly to me. It was a message of hope but I was struggling to respond to his altar call. I was told I could be baptized in water right then and there. Every time I tried to get up, something was holding me down.

Finally, I was able to get out of my seat. I ran down to the altar and I gave my life to Jesus Christ. I was baptized in Jesus' name. When I came out of the water of the baptismal pool, my nose was not dripping and my mind was not slipping. The shakes and body aches were gone.

I was so happy to be saved and set free. I shared the news as soon as I got home. When I woke up on New Year's Day, I was just happy and appreciative. I knew I had been released. I literally had no desire to use drugs. Before that night, when I woke up, I would always start each new day thinking about how and where I could find drugs.

A couple of weeks later, I received the precious gift of the Holy Ghost. I have never been to a rehab, detox or a 12-step program. I only made one step and that was into the house of the Lord. I never had any withdrawals or urges or desire to use drugs again. God took it all away at the church that night. My Jesus is a "habit breaker!"

However, I must admit that there were moments when I was afraid. I was still in the same environment with the same family members and friends who were users. I knew there would be a test to see if I could survive as a believer. But as of this writing, it has been 40 years since that glorious night. And I can bear witness to the saying, if you want to be kept, you can be kept!

There was real evidence that my life had changed. Before I got saved, some friends and I were looking for the guy who ripped me off for the cocaine I was selling. We finally ran into him while riding down Bergen Street in Newark. We all jumped out of the car and went to beat him up. He started crying and saying he didn't have the money and pleading for us not to hurt him. We let him go and I told him the next time I saw him, he had better have my money.

But the next time I saw him, I was saved and had turned my life around. All I could say to him was, "Jesus loves you."

Not only did Jesus Save My Soul, Jesus Saved My Life! Just about every time I would say the name Jesus in church, I would jump up and run around the church.

I was given the name "Road Runner."

Chapter 5

Saying "So Long" to Allah

I remember when I first got saved, some of my Muslim friends heard about it and came to my job. They told me that if I didn't denounce the name of Jesus, they would take back the name Naim Akbar Shabazz. They said, "You know what we've taught you; Allah is God and that the Honorable Elijah Mohammad was his last and greatest messenger."

I told those brothers that they could have the name Naim Akbar Shabazz because I had a name above every name and at the name of Jesus, every knee is going to bow and every tongue will confess that He is Lord.

A brother I used to run with came home from prison. At the time, he did not know I had given my life to Jesus. He got in touch with me, thinking I was that same old Naim. I invited him to attend church service with me and he agreed.

That night, the power of the Holy Ghost was really moving in the service. I began to shout and speak in tongues. My friend thought I had lost my mind and he immediately left the service. He put the word out on the street that I was crazy and had lost my mind.

I began to run into all my old Muslim friends and they had heard that I had given my life over to Jesus. They called me a Judas. I was talked about and made fun of. They said my change didn't mean nothing. They told me I was still a Muslim. When that didn't work, they all tried their best to get me to return to Islam.

They were relentless in coming after me. I must admit, at the beginning as a young Christian, the pressure was overbearing and I started to struggle with my decision. When I walked away from those encounters, it was one of the lowest parts of my life. Still, the scriptures helped me to stay strong and steadfast in my walk with the Lord.

After I got saved, the Lord blessed me to get my job back at General Motors. They offered to re-hire me. One day after I returned, I was drinking coffee. I set it down while working. Someone put drugs in my coffee. The world believes once an addict, always an addict. I noticed that everyone around me was staring and laughing at me, waiting for me to have a reaction from the drugs. I began to feel a little fearful and that's when the Lord dropped a scripture in my mind. It was Mark 16:18 which says, *"If they drink any deadly thing it shall not hurt them."*

That had to be the Lord because I had never read that scripture.

Chapter 6

The First Time I Gave My Testimony

"And when he was come into the ship, he that had been possessed with the devil prayed him that he might be with him. Howbeit, Jesus suffered him not, but saith unto him, **Go home to thy friends, and tell them what great things the Lord hath done for thee,** *and hath had compassion on thee. And he departed and began to publish in Decapolis what great things Jesus had done for him; and all men did marvel."* Mark 5:18-20 (emphasis added)

This scripture in the gospels tell how Jesus instructed the demonic man to go back to those who knew him and tell them how he had been delivered from his life of torment.

I will never forget when my cousin, Evangelist Carolyn Webb, our New Jersey State Council of the Pentecostal Assemblies of the World Young People President was invited to preach at the Pennsylvania State

Council. Before she preached, she called me up to give my testimony. I was so nervous because the place was packed out and I didn't know what I was going to say.

I thank God for the Holy Ghost! The Lord Jesus Christ took over and told me what to say. The Lord anointed me and used me in a mighty way. After my testimony, Evangelist Webb didn't preach; she just made an altar call for salvation.

One night, I was in our Thursday night prayer service at Faith Temple New Hope Church in East Orange, NJ. I was attending that church and it was there that the Lord spoke to me and told me I was to preach the Gospel of Jesus Christ. I responded, "Yes, Lord. I will preach your word." After prayer, I immediately went to my pastor. He said he had heard me answer the Lord in prayer saying, "Yes, I will preach your word."

One month after I heard the voice of the Lord, I was given the opportunity to preach my trial sermon. My first sermon was "Look at Me, Christ Has Set Me Free!" I was ordained by the New Jersey District Council in 1993.

My ministry was not limited to church services. I would share my testimony in tent revivals, prisons, halfway homes and nursing homes – wherever a door was opened. The Lord gave me holy boldness and I went forth. I believe that outreach was at the center of my gifting and anointing. Through the love of God, I was able to minister to people who many -- even church members -- felt were "undesirables."

Chapter 7

Mama, Can I Preach to You?

...a foolish son is the heaviness of his mother." Proverbs 10:1b

I don't think there was anyone in the world who appreciated the transformation in my life more than my mother, Anna Kornegay. She was a humble, quiet woman who did the best she could with what she had and we wanted for nothing. She worked as a neighborhood babysitter, keeping a number of children in our home.

Then, there was me. I was given the nickname Peewee: I never knew why. According to my mother, I always was a very bad child growing up. My rebellious behavior started at a very early age. I didn't like the fact that I had to be home or at least on the front porch by a certain time at night. I was stubborn to a fault and had my share of fights and truancy in those early years.

I was still living with my mother well into adulthood and only paid her $25 per week and barely could pay that because of my addiction. It broke her heart to witness her son literally destroying his life. Whenever I wasn't at home at night, they lived in fear, expecting to get a phone call that I had overdosed. She took out life insurance policies on me and my siblings because she didn't expect us to live a long life. They were always happy when I walked through the door.

What made matters worse, other family members were also using drugs. My brother Glenn and my sister Sheila both died as a result of complications from their drug use. But my mother was a special woman. I believe that God gave her grace to deal with all of her family's addiction struggles.

But I know there were times when I drove my mother crazy. I was still living at home when I was deep in my drug pursuits. One night, I was upstairs in the bathroom shooting cocaine. My heart started beating so fast; I thought it was coming out of my chest. I ran out of the bathroom with the needle still in my arm, screaming, "I'm dying! I'm dying!" My mother rushed me to the hospital emergency room. The doctor shot me up with an elephant tranquilizer to calm me down. She knew what was going on and she was there to help me see another day.

When I gave my life to the Lord, it blessed her so much. She had been attending other churches (I think I might have gone with her as a youngster but I couldn't remember for sure). But she joined and became a member of my church for 14 years. I was so happy that my new life made her proud. Not everybody is fortunate to be able to pastor their mother. When she passed away in 2013 at the age of 85, I was happy that Mother Anna E. Kornegay lived long enough to see my life changed and I knew that I would see her again in Glory.

Chapter 8

Face to Face With My Father

I didn't have a relationship with my natural father at all. I never met him as a child or teenager. I didn't miss him because I never knew him. There were no Father's Day celebrations in our house growing up. I don't doubt for a moment that God has His hand on my life, even before I got saved. But looking back, I wonder how my life might have been different if he had been around.

One day, I came to the house and there he was. I was 27, married and saved at the time. I didn't know who he was. It was the first time me or my siblings had seen him. Someone had to tell me that was Theodore Kornegay, alias Snook. Here was the man whose name was on my birth certificate, the man who had given me my last name.

I was shocked and upset. I thought about all the years my mother had struggled by herself. I felt like asking him, "Where have you been?" but I didn't. He had heard of my past reputation out on the streets. He asked me where he could find drugs!

He would come to the house almost every day after that and sit on the couch, watching television. Once in a while, he would talk to one of my sisters. He never said anything to me about my being in ministry.

He had moved away to Chicago years before. The rumor was that he was running from child support because he had babies everywhere. He had come back to New Jersey because he had sisters living here.

About a year later, in 1993, he passed away. They say he died of old age. I only saw him a couple of times right before he died. I had gone to visit him at the hospital.

Only family members were there at his funeral service. I have to be truthful; I didn't cry.

■■

"...thou art a helper of the fatherless." Psalm 10:14b

I had experienced one of the plagues of the African-American community. The absence of responsible men in the family structure has continued to devastate generations of households. The epidemic of absent fathers in today's society is vastly increasing and getting worst. Nearly 2 in 3 African American children live in a father-absent home.

Here's another perspective. According to the U.S. Census Bureau, "There is a crisis in America: 19.7 million children live without a father in the home. Consequently, there is a "father factor" in nearly all of the societal ills facing America today. Research shows when a child is raised in a father-absent home, he or she can be affected in the following ways:

- They have a four times greater risk of poverty;
- They are more likely to have behavioral problems;
- They are two times more likely to have a risk of infant mortality;
- They are more likely to go to prison;
- They are more likely to commit crimes;
- They are seven times more likely to become pregnant as a teen;
- They are more likely to face abuse and neglect;
- **They are more likely to abuse drugs and alcohol**;
- They are two times more likely to suffer obesity;
- They are two times more likely to drop out of high school."

Dr. Tony Evans, author of the *Kingdom Man* book and teaching series on biblical manhood, describes fatherlessness "as the scourge of our time. It's devastating for a number of reasons. First of all, it is a key element to the breakdown of the family, and the family is key to the well-being of society and social order. So when families break down, you have a lot of repercussions."

There is a role that the church can and should play to stand in the gap for young boys and girls who are missing the absence of a male figure at home. I trust brothers throughout the body of Christ will join me in reversing this generational curse. We can make a difference.

Chapter 9

I've Preached and Testified on Good Ground

"Also I heard the voice of the Lord, saying, Whom shall I send, and who will go for us? Then said I, Here am I, send me." Isaiah 6:8

My testimony would open doors for me to speak to churches and other groups more than I ever would have imagined. The Lord has blessed me to preach from the east coast to the west coast. Each time, I was given the opportunity to share my testimony. I can't recall a time where I've preached or given my testimony at conventions, revivals or conferences and a person didn't come to the altar to receive a life-changing experience: To God Be the Glory! When I left and went back home, I always had another person added to my counseling list.

I try my best to be transparent when I stand before people to share my life story. There's a song the Clark

Sisters sing that says *"It should have been me, it could have been me, it would have been me, if it wasn't for the Blood."*

Well, it was me and I'm not ashamed to tell it everywhere I go. Grace kept me and mercy covered me. Thank God for the Blood and I'm living to tell the Good News of Jesus Christ. Looking at my background, some might feel that I'm not worthy to preach. But I identify with two gospel songs and I will say this: *"I'm so glad Jesus looked beyond all my faults and saw my need." "I'm so glad Jesus loved me through my good and He loved me through my bad."*

I quickly learned that staying around the saints in the house of the Lord was necessary to keep strong. I even joined the choir despite the fact that I couldn't sing a lick. I hung around my pastor's house as much as I could. I was aware of the dangers of the environment that had surrounded me with temptations I couldn't resist. I was staying in church as much as possible to keep away from the world I was determined to leave behind.

My journey as a young preacher was supported by many, especially my wife, Sandra. One of my sisters, Lorraine was also very helpful. She allowed me to use her car to get to church when I didn't have my own transportation. I am grateful to so many other folks who encouraged me and helped me in ways, both big and small.

My ministry has always focused on people others may have felt were "undesirables." But James 2:3 exhorts us not to have respect of persons when people we may deem not the most desirable come into our places of worship. Having been out on the streets for years, I understood the downtrodden. That's why I witnessed to anyone and everyone I could.

Over the years, I witnessed a lot of addicts come in and get a "spiritual fix" and stay for a while until they felt strong. Then, they would go out until they had been weakened and come back in and get another fix. It was like a revolving door.

I preached a message that simply said, *"You Have a Future, Regardless of Your Past."*

Chapter 10

I'm Doing What I Love!

"...Do the work of an evangelist, make full proof of thy ministry." II Timothy 4:5a

Living Water New Life Ministries, the church I pastor is very non-traditional. Many come from near and far to hear my testimony and I still have to remain in a pastoral frame of mind. However, the Lord always managed to allow my testimony to line up with the Word of God.

Because of my testimony and my past life, many have been delivered from drugs, alcohol, cigarettes or other addictions and given their lives over to Jesus Christ. A faithful few have remained with our ministry. Like most churches, many others came to visit, some even joined, but they were not committed. Some drug addicts came but church was a revolving door for them. They would come and stay for a spiritual fix but leave after a while. They didn't want to separate from their past life and struggled to leave their past life behind.

Our church has been located in two cities in New Jersey. We first started out in Rahway, which is dominated by mostly Baptist churches. We became members of the Rahway Churches Alliance. This allowed me to give my testimony to Baptist, Catholic, Episcopalian, Methodist and AME churches. I became a sought-after advocate for drug prevention. And many pastors and members of these different churches would reach out to me to counsel their friends and family members.

One day, one of the Baptist pastors preached at a fellowship service at my church. I was stunned when he gave his topic for his message, which was "Wake up, Rahway! There's a real preacher in town named Leon Kornegay." He went on to say that there were serious issues in the town that had been ignored, but God sent in Pastor Kornegay to wake us up. I must say that fellowship service was an endorsement of acceptance in that community.

When I was in services at the Emmanuel Church of Christ in Newark, my pastor, Bishop James D. Churchwell would sometimes call on me to give my testimony. The church was in a very challenging neighborhood and drug users who came inside would hear me share my story right in the services. If they never heard about the delivering power of God ever again, I was able to let them know that I was a living example that there was an answer to their addictions.

The Lord was dealing with me concerning the location of Living Water New Life Ministries. It was the church I pastored and was originally in Rahway under the former Pastor John Wilson. When Pastor Wilson had transitioned, our Council sent associate ministers from various churches to preach on Sundays. Eventually, I was selected as the interim pastor, and then voted by the congregation to be the permanent pastor. The church membership was very small but the Lord blessed the ministry to grow. However, like most churches, it became a revolving door. I continued to seek the Lord in prayer asking, "Is this where I belong?"

I was thinking in terms of being a pastor because I love evangelism. Through much fasting and prayer, along with my wife, it was confirmed that my season in Rahway was up and my ministry must move forward. In Rahway, there were so many restrictions for religious groups because of certain city ordinances.

The Lord allowed us to relocate the church to Perth Amboy, NJ. It was there that so many doors began to open for my ministry. Now, I was doing what I love so much: "Outreach Ministry." Perth Amboy is very diverse with many shelters and homeless people to evangelize. And we were taking Christ to the streets. In the first two months, over 20 souls were baptized in Jesus' name. Perth Amboy is predominantly a Spanish speaking town. Our church connected with many Hispanic churches in the city and that has been a blessing. The Lord has blessed us with many bilingual members to help in the ministry.

Chapter 11

A Man after God's Own Heart

For if a man know not how to rule his own house, how shall he take care of the church of God? 1 Timothy 3:5

I must admit it. I had a lot of rough edges. I was stubborn to a fault. I had no clue how to be a husband or a father. Like many in the African American community, I had no role model to pattern my life after. I knew how to do church and I must admit that sometimes, I got carried away with the effect my testimony and my preaching had wherever I went. I wanted to be in church every time I could and didn't consider how my zeal was affecting my wife and then my children.

I guess I was aware of how many successful people in ministry had problems – sometimes major problems – at home. Some nationally known pastors were divorced because their wives finally gave up trying to compete with their ministry. Someone said that those ministers allowed the church to become their "spiritual mistress." Not everyone can undertake the mantle of a marriage that reflects the relationship between Christ and the church.

In fact, I was at risk because I didn't think a failed marriage could happen to me. But thank God for Sandra Kornegay. She had been in church all of her life and she was just what I needed. We might have seemed like opposites and in many respects we were. I came from the streets and she was brought up knowing God in a personal way. But we were determined through the grace of God to make it work.

Sandra and I struggled a lot during the first years of our marriage. But we were able to grow our relationship and God blessed us to remain committed to Him so that He would get the glory out of our marriage.

In setting priorities, the pastor must remember that it should be God first, family second and church next. When preachers are "on fire for God," that set of priorities gets lost. I was learning these truths as I worked to grow my faith and be a blessing to those I went home to be with when church was over.

I was well aware of the problem of generational curses and when my two sons were born, I was committed to see them grow up with a positive role model they could call daddy. I knew I had to set an example in my home and even to those men I led in our congregation and encountered in the community.

As a pastor, I was well aware that strong marriages and strong families feed into strong churches. There's no doubt that Satan realizes if he can keep discord in the home, he can impact the effectiveness of the body of Christ. The attacks on the institution of marriage have been relentless. When we learn that there are almost as many divorces among church members, we can see why so many marriage seminars and retreats are being held to help couples to remain together and work on their marriages. Saints are called on to represent Christ – single or married. Far too many are willing to throw in the towel and forget those vows they made before God and man: "Until death do us part."

Wedding Day 1981

Lady Sandra and Pastor Leon Kornegay

Mother Anna E. Kornegay

Pastor praying during street ministry

Leon Kornegay in 9th grade yearbook

Preaching the Word

Brothers Ron Kornegay and Leon Kornegay

Leon and his offspring

Kornegay siblings with their spouses and sister

Bishop Joseph Allen and Evangelist Beverly Allen with Pastor Kornegay

Chapter 12

It's All about Souls

"Whatsoever thy hand findeth to do, do it with thy might..." Ecclesiastes 9:10

I was blessed with a special love for helping mankind.

Someone said that the greatest ministry is one-on-one ministry. Part of my testimony is that I worked as a drug and alcohol counselor. My testimony opened doors for me to begin a counseling ministry, providing support to individuals with any kind of addiction. My life resonated with people, young and old, who knew I had been in their shoes and found deliverance in Jesus Christ.

In addition to my pastoral responsibilities, I was a counselor at a halfway house, preparing convicts for a second chance in society for five years. In addition, I was a Substance Abuse Counselor for 10 years at a Detox and Methadone clinic.

Before my retirement on June 30, 2018, I was employed as a Life Skills Instructor at an alternative high school for 11 years, working with young people dealing with addictions and other problems. Many of them had been abused. Members of the infamous gangs, the Bloods or the Crips were students there. Some of the girls were pregnant or had children. But the classes were smaller and despite the challenges, there were success stories.

It was a great blessing anytime one of those young people graduated and turned their lives around. Some went on to college or furthered their education at culinary schools.

Chapter 13

Raising Children in the Opioid Era

"Train up a child in the way he should go: and when he is old, he will not depart from it." Proverbs 22:6

Down through the years, parents have asked how to prevent their children for succumbing to the temptation to use illegal drugs. Some parents are stunned when they feel they have done everything right and a child still goes on drugs. It is absolutely vital to be vigilant as a parent.

Addiction doesn't happen overnight. All too often, warning signs were missed. What are some of the warning signs?

- The child becomes isolated and more quiet than usual;
- start coming home later than in previous times;
- becomes evasive when questioned;

- becomes rebellious and defiant.

There are others, but it is imperative to know your child and watch for unexplained behaviors.

At the time of this writing, over two million persons suffer from opioid addiction. In 2016, 42,000 Americans lost their lives, more than any previous year on record. While abuse of prescription drugs is gaining most of the headlines, heroin and cocaine still pose a danger. And they are considered under the umbrella of opioids.

The problems in our culture are manifesting in Christian homes. Children are often the most vulnerable. There is no way to control what is going on in society so every effort must be made in the home to counteract the influences children face. The temptations are real. Peer pressure is real. Since we know the source of evil, we must engage in spirited warfare for the lives of the next generation. Looking back, my path to addiction started with taking pills.

I will summarize my advice:

- Pray over your child daily, from conception (yes, conception) and especially after they are born;

- Make a commitment to spend quality time with your family and bond with your children to make positive lifelong memories.
- Teach your child the things of the Lord through their own Children's Bible and Christian videos. Take them to church on a regular basis;
- Have a baby dedication or christening for your child in infancy;
- Set an example by allowing your child see you pray in the home;
- Have regular family devotions in your home and teach your child to say grace and to pray;
- Have family rules for the home and standards of behavior;
- Use appropriate but fair discipline when necessary;
- Have a standard for television programming and internet usage. Carefully monitor video game purchases (they have ratings);
- Work to have your child trust you enough to share anything and everything with you;
- Encourage your child to bring friends over to your home so that you can observe the children he or she chooses to call their friends;

- If your child spends time with another friend at their home, get to know the parents and make a decision on whether that seems to be a good environment for your child;
- Check your child's room from time to time to determine if there is anything that suggests they may be disobeying your rules and instructions;
- Look for signs of changed behavior that may be the first indication of a problem;
- Seek help (Pastor, youth leader, Christian counselor or written resources) when you are confronting a challenge and you are unsure of what path to take.

Addendum

Survivor of the Year Award
Presented to Pastor Leon Kornegay
By: Got Vision
February 11, 2019

Ras J. Baraka
MAYOR
NEWARK, NEW JERSEY

Presented To
Pastor Leon Kornegay
Survivor of the Year Award
February 11, 2019

As Mayor of the City the City of Newark, it is my pleasure to congratulate you as you are being honored by Got Vizion Inc. I pray for you to have a blessed day of celebration as you are celebrated and so well deserving of this honor.

I applaud you Pastor Leon Kornegay for your diligence and devotion to promoting excellence in spiritual leadership. We are proud to acknowledge you for the many contributions you have made and for the strong foundation of spiritual and ethical values that you have built in the surrounding community and the many lives you have touched though your ministry.

I know you will continue to be an inspiration to us all, and that your greatest days are in front of you. May God continue to keep the gift that you are and will continue to be. Thank you for making a difference in the lives of others and may this day be a most memorable one.

God Bless You,

Ras J. Baraka,
Mayor

City of Newark, N.J.

The Newark Municipal Council hereby issues this Resolution

Commending

Pastor Leon Kornegay

Survivor of the Year Award

We, the Members of the Newark Municipal Council, proudly recognize and commend you on being honored at the Third Annual Pastors' Ball, "A Night of Elegance" to celebrate and honor servants who have faithfully extended their time and humble service to "Serve This Present Age, Their Calling to Fulfill", at the Park Savoy Estates, located in Florham Park, New Jersey, on Monday, February 11, 2019. May you continue to fulfill your Kingdom Assignments in the Church, the Community and the Marketplace respectively.

Mildred C. Crump
PRESIDENT, MUNICIPAL COUNCIL

Augusto Amador
COUNCIL MEMBER

LaMonica R. McIver
COUNCIL MEMBER

Carlos M. Gonzalez
COUNCIL MEMBER

Eddie Osborne
COUNCIL MEMBER

John Sharpe James
COUNCIL MEMBER

Luis A. Quintana
VICE PRESIDENT - MUNICIPAL COUNCIL

Joseph A. McCallum, Jr.
COUNCIL MEMBER

Anibal Ramos Jr.
COUNCIL MEMBER

Attest: _Kenneth Louis_   Date: _February 11, 2019_
Kenneth Louis
City Clerk